Library of Congress Cataloging-in-Publication Data

Watts, Barrie.
    Apple tree.

    (Stopwatch books)
    Includes index.
    Summary: Describes in simple text and illustrations
how an apple develops from a blossom in the spring
to a ripe fruit in the autumn.
    1. Apple — Juvenile literature. 2. Apple —
Reproduction — Juvenile literature. [1. Apple]
I. Title. II. Series.
QK495.R78W38   1987   583.372   86-31500
ISBN 0-382-09440-9
ISBN 0-382-09436-0 (lib. bdg.)

First published by A & C Black (Publishers) Limited
35 Bedford Row, London WC1R 4JH

© 1986 Barrie Watts

Published in the United States in 1987
by Silver Burdett Press,
Morristown, New Jersey

Acknowledgements
The artwork is by Helen Senior
The publishers would like to thank Jean Imrie for her help and advice.

Apple Tree

Barrie Watts

Stopwatch books

Silver Burdett Press • Morristown, New Jersey

Here are some apples.

Do you like to eat apples? You can see lots of different kinds at a fruit stand. They all have different colors and tastes.

All these apples grew the same way. They grew on trees in an orchard like this one.

This book will tell you how apples grow.

In winter the apple tree has no leaves.

Here is an apple tree in winter. It has no leaves or fruit. You can see the shape of its branches.

The tree rests through the winter. When the weather gets warmer, buds begin to grow on the tips of the branches.

Look at the big photograph. Inside each bud there are tiny leaves. They are folded up and ready to open.

In spring the leaves open.

Soon the tiny leaves begin to unfold. They are bright green and about the size of your thumbnail. As the leaves grow bigger, they get darker in color.

The tree needs light, water, and air so that it can live and grow.

The roots of the tree spread out under the ground to collect water. The leaves open to get as much light as they can. The tree gets air through tiny holes in its leaves and branches.

The apple tree has flowers.

When the leaves have opened, flower buds start to grow at the ends of the twigs. As the weather gets warmer, the flowers begin to open. Look at this photograph.

Can you see the petals beginning to unfold?

Look at the big photograph. By late spring, most of the flowers have opened. The flowers on an apple tree are usually called blossoms.

Bees visit the flowers.

Here is an open flower.

Around the outside of the flower there are five petals.
In the middle there are lots of tiny stalks. The tops of the
stalks are covered with a special yellow dust called pollen.

On a sunny day, bees visit the flowers to look for food.
Look at the big photograph. When a bee crawls inside the
flower, it gets pollen on its body. Can you see the
yellow blobs of pollen on the bee's legs?

A tiny apple starts to grow.

When the bee goes to the next flower, some of the pollen on its body brushes off inside the flower. When this happens, a tiny apple may start to grow.

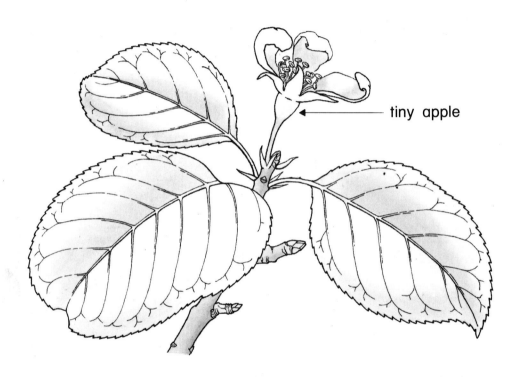

tiny apple

A tiny apple is growing behind the petals of this flower.

Now look at the photograph. As the apple grows bigger, the flower dries up and the petals fall off.

The apple grows bigger.

The tiny apple has been growing for two weeks.
It is getting bigger and rounder.

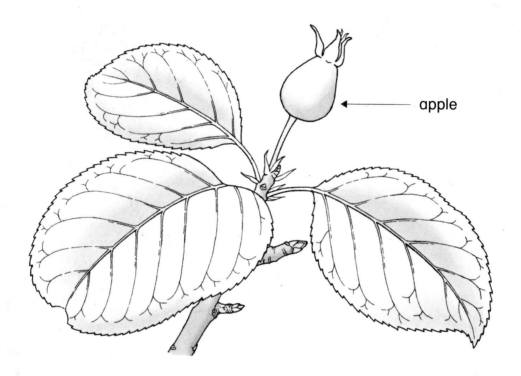

apple

Look at the photograph. After four weeks the apple is as
big as a golf ball. It is quite hard and tastes very sour.

Can you see the dried up parts of the flower on top
of the fruit?

The apple is ready to pick.

All summer the apple keeps growing. In autumn it is ripe. This apple is sweet and juicy, and parts of its skin have turned red.

Look at the big photograph. This apple has been cut in half. The middle of the apple is called the core. Inside the core, there are dark brown pits. The pits are the seeds of the apple tree.

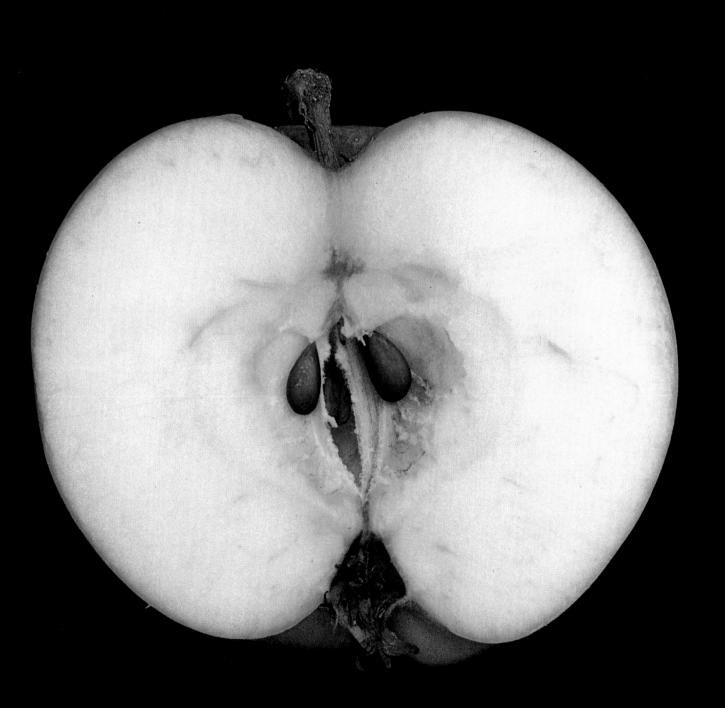

The apples fall off the tree.

The apples are heavy. When the wind blows, they fall off the tree. These apples are called windfalls. Look at the big photograph. Can you see the windfalls at the bottom of the tree?

Some of the windfalls are eaten. Others start to rot. This apple has mold growing on it.

When the apple rots, some of the pits may drop into the earth. Sometimes they may start to grow into tiny trees.

The leaves fall off the apple tree.

In late autumn, the apple tree grows much more slowly. The leaves dry up and change color. When the leaves have turned brown, they drop off the tree. A scar is left where each leaf used to be.

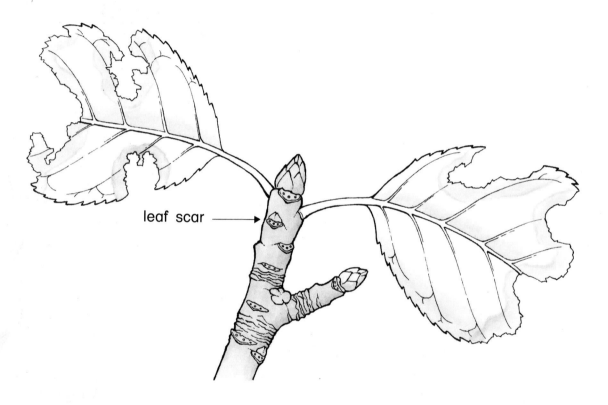

leaf scar

Soon the leaves will rot and be eaten by insects and worms.

The tree is bare.

Through the winter, the branches of the tree are bare again.

Some of the apples are still lying on the ground.
They are food for hungry animals and birds.
Look at the photograph. This apple is frozen solid,
but the starling has still eaten most of it.

Soon it will be spring. When the weather gets warmer,
buds will appear on the branches of the tree.
What do you think will happen then?

Do you remember how an apple grows?
See if you can tell the story in your own words.
You can use these pictures to help you.

3

6

Index

This index will help you to find some of the important words in the book.

apple 2, 12, 14, 16, 18
autumn 20

bee 10, 12
blossom 8
branch 4, 22
bud 4, 8, 22

core 16

flower 8, 10, 12, 14
fruit 14

leaf 4, 6, 20

orchard 2

petals 8, 10, 12
pits 16, 18
pollen 10, 12

ripe 16
roots 6
rot 18, 20

scar 20
spring 8, 22
summer 16

windfall 18
winter 4

You might like to keep a tree diary. Watch a tree change through the year. Then you can draw pictures and write about it.